Original title:
Peach and Light

Copyright © 2025 Creative Arts Management OÜ
All rights reserved.

Author: Lorenzo Barrett
ISBN HARDBACK: 978-1-80586-449-3
ISBN PAPERBACK: 978-1-80586-921-4

A Dance of Color and Warmth

In the orchard where giggles bloom,
Juicy orbs sway with laughter's tune.
Waltzing under the sun's bright gaze,
Fruitful pranks in the summer's haze.

With every splash of a sticky bite,
Silly faces in pure delight.
The blossoms wink like mischief today,
As the bees buzz in a playful fray.

Radiant Treasures Beneath the Canopy

Beneath the leaves, in shadows cast,
Mischief brews, so sweet and vast.
Tiny hands reach for the gold,
Secrets of summer in each fold.

Giggling squirrels join the fun,
While juicy gems bask in the sun.
A game of tag amongst the trees,
As laughter floats upon the breeze.

Sweet Sunset Serenade

When twilight spills its rosy flair,
The world turns soft, a warm affair.
Chasing fireflies that twirl and plead,
Their glowing dance is pure mischief indeed.

Whispered secrets of dusk delight,
As critters join for evening flight.
With every glow and every giggle,
Even shadows can't help but wiggle.

Lush Embrace of Summer's Gift

In the lushness of a lazy morn,
A tangled hornet's nest is born.
While we dare to reach with wobbly hands,
Joyful chaos in sun-kissed lands.

Bounding back from a tumble's cheer,
With juicy stains from ear to ear.
The day's embrace, a soft caress,
Where every moment is sheer success.

Citrus Dreams in Soft Sunbeam

In a grove where giggles grow,
The fruit wears a sunniest glow.
They dance on branches in a race,
A juicy smile on every face.

With playful zings in summer air,
The citrus chuckles everywhere.
They bounce like kids upon the grass,
While silly squirrels slyly pass.

The Glow of Juicy Days

When the sun beams with a grin,
And fruity faces start to spin.
A splash of zest, a wink, a tease,
Tickle the branches like a breeze.

Each droplet sparkles like a wink,
As laughter flows and thoughts all shrink.
The flavor fights for center stage,
In this sweet, absurd, golden age.

Orchard Whispers in the Breeze

Amidst the trees, the stories play,
 Of juicy treasures bright as day.
 A jester's cap upon each crown,
 They giggle softly, never frown.

The wind carries a ticklish tune,
 A serenade beneath the moon.
 Each rustle holds a secret laugh,
 Their zestful joy, a funny draft.

Basking in the Golden Hour

In twilight's glow, the laughter swells,
With every fruit, a tale it tells.
A funny face on every round,
As silliness can often be found.

So let us sip this juicy breeze,
And share our jokes beneath the trees.
In this warm hour, let's all play,
For bliss awaits in bright array.

Fruity Luminescence

In a bowl of chums, I saw a scene,
A fuzzy fellow with a wobbly sheen.
He wiggled and jiggled, big grin on his face,
"Come join the dance, let's pick up the pace!"

The banter kept going, the fruit with flair,
"You can call me fuzzy, but I'm sweet as air!"
Laughter erupted, they rolled on the floor,
"Where's my dessert? This party's a bore!"

Golden Hues on a Summer Day

Sunshine dipped in happiness, oh what a sight,
Bouncing and jiving, from morning till night.
Each round giggle bouncing, a fruity delight,
"I might squirt juice, but I'm really polite!"

With peals of laughter ricocheting high,
One twirled in a circle, reaching the sky.
"Don't squeeze me too tight, I'm not made of steel!"
And the fruit brigade laughed at their juicy appeal!

Sun-Kissed Moments

A group of sweet friends basking in cheer,
"Who's got the bowl? Let's spread some good cheer!"
They chuckled and giggled, all shades of gold,
"Dance with me now, you're too cute to scold!"

The sun spread its rays, a shimmering show,
As they tumbled and rolled, stealing the glow.
"Life's a party, don't forget your hat!"
Each laugh shared was a whimsical spat!

Radiance of the Orchard

In a whimsical orchard, the sun's got a grin,
Each fruit on the branch, ready to spin.
"I'm sweeter than sugar, and fuzzy to boot,"
Laughter erupted, a musical hoot!

They rested in shade with a pun or two,
"Hey! Who squished my buddy? Was that you?"
With giggles and snickers, they spun in a whirl,
"Let's throw a fruit party, give the sun a twirl!"

Whispering Glow of Nature

In the orchard where giggles fly,
Fruits chuckle as they ripen nigh.
A tree too wise with secrets spun,
Winks at folks just trying for fun.

Sunbeams tickle the boughs so round,
Nature's jesters all abound.
Rustling leaves sing a silly tune,
While bees shimmy in the afternoon.

A squirrel dreams of a fruity feast,
While birds are reading jokes at least.
Underneath the cheerful sway,
Every moment's a laugh-filled play.

Radiance Wrapped in Silk

Dressed in shades of golden swirl,
The fruits gather for a dance and twirl.
With peels like smiles and laughter loud,
They pull in critters from the crowd.

A windup squirrel starts to cheer,
As rabbits leap without a fear.
In this party, none hold back,
The colors burst, no hint of black.

Each bite a giggle, fresh delight,
While shadows join the playful sight.
With twinkling reflections that gleam and drift,
Nature wraps all in her playful gift.

Cherished Glow of Ephemeral Beauty

In moments bright, the world's a jest,
With nature dressed in vibrant zest.
Fragrant whispers fill the air,
As laughter dances everywhere.

Golden globes catch glimmers rare,
Joking with the breeze, with flair.
Petals chuckle, swaying slow,
Amidst the sparkle, life's a show.

Burst of joy hangs from each stem,
Cheeky hues, a precious gem.
Even shadows crack a smile,
Nature's humor spans a mile.

Soft Radiant Dreams

In a slumbering field, colors gleam,
Chasing rainbows feels like a dream.
With whimsy wrapped in every hue,
    Nature giggles in a soft debut.

A mischievous sun peeks and pouts,
While clouds tease the world with their shouts.
Butterflies flit in a ballet grand,
Tickling flowers, dancing hand in hand.

When night drapes stars like silly hats,
The moon beams winks at critters and mats.
Every moment a joyous chase,
    In this twilight of radiant grace.

Sun-Kissed Reverie

A fuzzy fruit danced on a vine,
It chuckled as it swayed in time.
Beneath the sun, it took a twirl,
With giggles, it made the garden whirl.

A bee passed by, wearing a hat,
Swapping jokes with a falling cat.
They laughed so hard, the leaves did shake,
While shadows played at a silly break.

Clarity in Warmth

A bright orb spills its citrus cheer,
As squirrels debate if they're out of beer.
A rabbit pranks with a hop and a wink,
While pondering just what cats might think.

The flowers bloom, and the colors shout,
While the grass whispers, 'What's this about?'
The breeze joins in with a playful dance,
Inviting the clouds to join in the prance.

Silken Warmth of the Earth

The soil chuckles as worms do glide,
Underneath, where secrets hide.
A ladybug wears a tiny crown,
As grass tickles feet, never a frown.

A sunbeam races through the leaves,
Playing tag with all that it weaves.
The daisies gossip in petal tails,
While a sleepy hedgehog dreams of trails.

Blazing Hues of Twilight

The sky blushes, a marvelous show,
As fireflies gear up for a glow.
A raccoon pranks in the fading light,
While stars await to join the night.

Colors clash like a carnival dance,
As shadows stretch, they take their chance.
The moon peeks out, with a cheeky grin,
Saying, 'Let the madness begin!'

Fruitful Radiance

A plump orb of twilight hangs,
Wobbling like a belly laugh.
It grins as raindrops dance,
Sugary whispers from the staff.

A pluck and a squish, oh what a thrill,
Nature's jester on the vine.
Drippy, sticky, oh what a spill,
A sweet surprise, oh-so-fine.

Sunny-faced and giggling bright,
Juicy morsels twinkle near.
The breeze jokes, 'What's shining tonight?'
A game of catch with cheer.

Chubby cheeks of citrus fun,
Ripe giggles tumble low.
Under the orchard, everyone,
Can't help but steal the show.

Soft Gleam of Harvest

In fields of chatter and cheeky charm,
Bouncing buds sway in time.
Each carry a sweetness, never harm,
As they hop along the rhyme.

Golden suns with a wink so wide,
A fruity festival in the air.
Frolicking fans cannot decide,
Which delighted bite to share.

With ticklish laughs and juicy spills,
Hilarity bursts with every munch.
Fruits project their fruity thrills,
Harvest joy packs a punch.

A gleam in eyes, a spirited game,
Who'll crunch first, it's unclear.
Laughter echoes, no one's to blame,
For tasting joy, oh hear, hear!

Sunkissed Petals

Drenched in whimsy, petals burst,
Round and rosy, feel the cheer.
Nature's candy, quenching thirst,
    Nibbles that pull you near.

With hues that giggle under trees,
Bright flutters in a sunny glow.
A round parade upon the breeze,
"Do take a bite!" they seem to crow.

    Sticky fingers, all aglow,
Sprinkled sparks of mirth abound.
A treasure trove of color flow,
    Laughter in each bite is found.

In twilight's grip, the fun won't cease,
The orchard hums with carefree talk.
    Every nibble is a feast,
As jubilant dancers walk the walk.

Golden Ember Euphoria

A bubbly burst of amber dreams,
Dancing in the summer's grasp.
Laughter rolls like flowing streams,
With giggles caught in every clasp.

Sweet honeyed giggles, sunny and bold,
Hiding in the grass with flair.
Stories of mischief unfold,
As joy bounces in the air.

A sunny kick, a playful tease,
What flavor tickles your tongue?
They're cheeky with their ease,
Each laugh a note that's sung.

Sipping happiness, we dive right in,
Outrageous fun, it's a beautiful spin.
Golden delights that spark a grin,
In this fruity frolic, we all win!

Gentle Flare of Memory

In a fruity haze, I trip and fall,
Bouncing on dreams like a beach ball.
A slice of laughter, juice on my chin,
I giggle at monkeys, inviting them in.

Sticky fingers dance, what a wild scene,
Stumbling through gardens, so lush and green.
A chuckle erupts with every sweet bite,
Forgetfulness drapes me in amber light.

Dazzling Cove of Joy

In sunlit corners where giggles explode,
Mischievous critters glance down the road.
A splash of color, a wink of the eye,
I pluck at a fruit, then it goes awry.

Swirling confetti from trees up above,
Each silly tumble feels filled with love.
The laughter we harvest, the joy that we glean,
We've all lost our hats in this vibrant scene.

Warmth Beneath the Canopy

Under the leaves, where the silliness reigns,
Twisting like vines in absurd little chains.
I trip on a root while telling a tale,
And the squirrels all giggle, they're quite the detail.

With rays through the branches, it's all quite a mess,
Each bump and each laugh is a playful caress.
In the snickers of nature, we find our delight,
While dreaming of snacks that are silky and bright.

Pastel Mirage of Dream

In pastel clouds where the wild things play,
A dance of mischief with sunshine all day.
Caught in a whirl of soft, fuzzy bliss,
I trip on a giggle, what did I miss?

With each funny blunder, the colors just twirl,
Like candy confetti in a whimsical whirl.
We nap in the cool, where the sweet breezes flow,
Wrapped in a chuckle, no hint of woe.

Summer's Tender Embrace

In a fruit bowl bright, a sight to see,
Squishy delights, a joy to me.
Chasing shadows, laughing loud,
Sticking stickers on a sunny cloud.

Wiggling toes in warm, soft sand,
Sipping sweet juice, it's simply grand.
A funny dance with bees up high,
While ants resolve to still deny.

When a breeze flips hats, oh what a chase,
Sun-kissed cheeks, a bright smile on face.
Tickling the sun with playful zeal,
As laughter echoes, it's quite the deal.

Warm Hues of Morning

Mornings burst with a vibrant glow,
Fragrant giggles, as laughter flows.
Over pancakes stacked, syrup on top,
A sweet tumble, oh help, don't stop!

Birds start singing a silly tune,
Dancing in circles around a big spoon.
A splash of juice, a tart surprise,
Sticky fingers and wide-open eyes.

A sunbeam prances, slips on a shoe,
Chasing the cat, oh what will it do?
Morning mischief in golden rays,
Waking up dreams in quirky ways.

Citrus Daydream

In a land where lemons do tango and twist,
Peeling giggles, you can't resist.
Dancing with oranges, such zest they share,
Juggling fruits in the sun's warm glare.

Cute little limes march in a line,
Every round trip is just divine.
Silly songs in the juicy breeze,
Lemonade laughter flows with ease.

Cracking up at the fruit stand scene,
Waiting for taste, a smile unseen.
A citrus comedy, oh what a show,
With wizards of zest putting on a glow!

Luminous Blossom's Serenade

Up in the trees, a bloom's delight,
Spreading smiles in the warm daylight.
Petals giggle as the wind blows by,
A floral ballet underneath the sky.

Buzzy bees buzz, making quite the fuss,
Whirling around, they need more than us.
Dance with the daisies, trip on the grass,
Nature's chuckle, as moments pass.

With every flutter, a chuckle follows,
Witty whispers amidst light swallows.
Blooming laughter in fragrant air,
A whimsical journey, life without care.

Hues of Nectar and Sunshine

In a grove where giggles grow,
The fruit hangs low, just like my woe.
A squirrel takes aim at my hat,
I yell, "That's not where snacks are at!"

Golden orbs and fuzzy skin,
I chase the son in a comical spin.
With each bite, juice down my chin,
Who knew eating could be such a win?

Dancing bees, they do their thing,
As I trip over my own string.
Laughter rings with every slip,
A classic scene, what a tasty trip!

With every squish and splat on toes,
A tasty mess, as everyone knows.
I'll take this fun in the sun's warm rays,
And count the giggles of these sweet days.

Glow of Ripened Joy

Skies so bright, they're blushing too,
As fruit turns gold, just like my shoe.
With sticky fingers, what a sight,
Who doesn't love a fruit-filled fight?

Wobbling dance with treasure in hand,
A challenge met, do you understand?
Fruits bounce back, my cart's a sight,
Rolling downhill, oh, what a flight!

Unexpected trips, a tumble or two,
Land in a patch, all covered in dew.
This orchard's filled with laughter and cheer,
Splat! A berry lands right near my ear!

In every bite, a giggle lingers,
As nature paints with happy fingers.
I'll savor this joy from the eve till morn,
In sweetness found, I was reborn!

Warm Embrace of Serene Days

On lazy afternoons, the sun spills gold,
A treasure map of stories untold.
Carts full of fruits, they roll and sway,
As we chase our shadows, no worries today!

Juicy bites spark chuckles galore,
While one fruit thief sneaks out the door.
A cheeky grin as they make a break,
With sticky truths, can you trust a snake?

Whispers of fruit in a warm, soft breeze,
Tickling my senses with such sweet tease.
Jousting with friends, using snacks as a shield,
With every bite, another laugh revealed!

Days like these, fresh sun on the skin,
Who knew life's battles were better with gin?
A slice of laughter, a slather of cheer,
In a world so sweet, there's nothing to fear!

Sunset and Orchard's Bounty

As the day dips low, colors collide,
In the orchard's arms, I take my ride.
Wobbling home with bags so heavy,
An apple rolls out, oh, what a levee!

Sunset spills like juice on my shirt,
A squishy bounty amidst the dirt.
Laughter rings out, a carousel ride,
Around the trunk, where secrets hide.

Friends toss fruits like frisbees in the air,
I'm the target! Quite a sticky affair.
With laughter ringing, we all make bets,
Who'll catch the most? The biggest regrets!

As stars wake up, giggles remain,
In this orchard, we dance in the rain.
With memories made and stories to tell,
This twilight glow, our treasure, our spell!

Dawn's Embrace

The sun wakes up with a yawn,
As shadows stretch on the lawn.
Birds chirp tunes in a cheeky way,
Morning giggles start the day.

In pajamas of sleepy hue,
I trip on toe socks, oh boo!
Coffee spills with a splashy splat,
A dance with my cat, imagine that!

Fluffy clouds play hide and seek,
While squirrels chatter, oh so cheeky.
Butterflies aim for my nose, oh dear,
This hilarious start, I hold it near.

With the world wrapped in joy's embrace,
Each moment brings a silly face.
Chasing breezes, I skip and sway,
Dawn's embrace makes me want to play.

Captivating Ember's Dance

A firefly winks in the dark,
While crickets play their evening lark.
The glow around is soft and warm,
Bringing nature's laugh and charm.

Bumblebees buzz with a swagger,
Dancing round like a double dagger.
They trip on petals, such a sight,
Their tango adds to the night's delight.

Stars join in with a twinkling jig,
While owls hoot, making it big.
A marshmallow dreams of melting flight,
S'mores giggle, oh what a bite!

The ember's dance, a comical tease,
With laughter swirling on the breeze.
In this moment, joy will prance,
Under the stars, we take our chance.

Luminance of Soft Midday

The sun is high, the sky is blue,
With ice cream cones long overdue.
Kids run wild with sticky hands,
Creating chaos in sunbathed lands.

Squirrels plot a nutty prank,
As lemonade fills up my tank.
A clothespin slips in my hair,
Then suddenly, I'm a fashion flare!

Kites take flight, so bold and bright,
Yet they tangle in a playful fight.
Laughter echoes as they swoop,
Everyone joins in the silly loop.

Heat waves shimmer on the ground,
In this bliss, pure joy is found.
With midday giggles in the sun,
Life's a game, and we all have fun.

Gentle Fusion of Nature

Breezes toss leaves in silly spins,
Nature whispers, then bursts into grins.
Flowers sway in a friendly row,
Laughing at bees that steal the show.

Frogs croak jokes from the bog,
As turtles waddle like a fog.
A gopher pops up, lets out a cheer,
He jiggles around, spreading good cheer.

Raindrops pattern on a tin roof,
Each one a tap, a dance, a hoof.
Puddles splash with playful sounds,
As laughter leaps on muddy grounds.

With trees serving up their leafy shade,
This gentle fusion of fun is made.
In every corner where we roam,
Nature's humor brings us home.

Enveloping Warmth

In a world so ripe and round,
Sunshine dances on the ground.
Fuzzy skin with a giggle bright,
Creating laughter, pure delight.

Every bite spills juicy cheer,
Taste buds singing, loud and clear.
Silly faces, messy grins,
A sticky joy, where fun begins.

We share a slice, just don't be shy,
If it drips, let out a cry!
Swirling around in sweet surprise,
In this silly moment, joy arises.

So gather 'round, let's have some fun,
Under the warm, bright sun.
With a fruit that brings such glee,
Life's a comic jubilee!

Dreamy Shades of Warm Embrace

There's a glow in the afternoon,
Like giggles that just chase the moon.
Chubby cheeks and mischievous eyes,
In the air, a playful surprise.

Whispers of dreams float up high,
As we toss them against the sky.
Colors dance, all pickled and bright,
Tickling the funny bone, what a sight!

Each moment's a palette of cheer,
With every smile, we draw near.
We leap and bound in joyful chase,
In this funny, warm embrace.

So let's clink our sweetie cups,
In this realm where laughter erupts.
Floating in hues, so whimsical and wild,
Life tastes as sweet as a happy child!

Hues of Bouncing Light

Sprinkled sunshine, like confetti,
Bouncing laughter, oh so petty.
A swirl of colors on a platter,
Every glance, a giggle, splatter!

Saffron splashes, tangerine twist,
A fruity whirl, too good to resist.
Giggling joy with every bite,
Caution: it may take flight!

So let's roll in this vibrant fun,
Who knew eating could weigh a ton?
With flavors that make your toes dance,
This is one wild, joyous romance!

In this circus of taste and cheer,
All our worries disappear.
Let's embrace the colorful spree,
And keep the fun rolling, whee!

Lush Hues of Daybreak

A round fruit rolls on the floor,
It giggles as it asks for more.
With colors bright and smiles wide,
It dances under morning's guide.

The squirrel tries to catch a ride,
But trips and tumbles, swells with pride.
The sun peeks in, a golden tease,
As nature joins the playful glees.

The dew drops glisten, a playful race,
The flowers sway, they quicken their pace.
A honeybee buzzes, oh what a sight,
Bumping blooms, it's pure delight.

And here we laugh, at the funny show,
As the world wakes up, in a bright, warm glow.

Gilded Echoes of Bliss

A fruity laugh rang loud and clear,
With every bite, we shed a tear.
It's sweet absurdity, that we embrace,
With giggles ringing through the space.

A fuzzy critter steals a treat,
With a waddle that can't be beat.
It hiccups twice, then takes a dance,
While trees all whisper, 'Give it a chance!'

The berries blush in morning's glow,
While friends swap tales of woe and flow.
With every chuckle, the day unfolds,
In hues of laughter, bright and bold.

So gather round, embrace the fun,
In gilded echoes, we have won.

Candlelit Sunrise

A sleepy fruit in morning's light,
Stumbles out from the cozy night.
The world ignites with a playful yawn,
As shadows stretch, it's time to dawn.

With giggling flames in jars aglow,
They chatter softly, putting on a show.
The walls dance joyfully, swaying around,
While whispers tell of the day we've found.

A toast to the sun, with a clink and cheer,
A nostalgia for days we hold dear.
Each laugh a flicker, each smile a spark,
As we bask in the warmth until it turns dark.

So let the candles guide our way,
For funny tales always save the day.

Warm Embrace of Fuzzy Dreams

The fuzzballs laugh, in a huddled heap,
With giggles that tickle, they start to leap.
A pillow plump, a hammock sway,
As dreams unfold in a cheeky play.

The sun pokes in, a warm embrace,
While sleepyheads wear silly face.
A symphony of snorts and squeals,
Awakening joy, as laughter reels.

They roll and tumble, in a feathery pile,
Trading funny looks, and every style.
With giggles spilling into the streams,
Life's a cozy box of fuzzy dreams.

So here we snuggle, and chuckles swell,
In a dreamland where all is well.

Day's End Lullaby

As the sun takes a dive,
Belly-flopping on the sea,
Silly shadows start to jive,
Dancing like they're carefree.

The sky turns pink, a light show,
Cows wear shades and sip some tea,
The breeze begins to blow slow,
Whispering jokes from a bee.

Grasshoppers play a funny tune,
While daisies join in with glee,
Under the glowing moon,
Crickets hum a melody.

Stars peek out, oh what a chat,
They gossip about the day,
Winking like a friendly cat,
As night steals the light away.

Sweet Incandescence

Berries laugh on a vine,
Telling tales of summer's brew,
Sugarplum clouds, oh so fine,
Whip up a whimsical view.

Ripe laughter fills the warm air,
As colors cascade in a swirl,
Fruit flies dance, without a care,
Swaying in a dizzy whirl.

Bumblebees in tiny suits,
Play hopscotch on the breeze,
With sprightly boots and funny hoots,
They tease the tiptoeing trees.

Sunshine giggles, watches still,
As raindrops crack a cheeky grin,
A fruit-filled banquet on the hill,
Where the fun and joy begin.

Gentle Hues of Sunset

Orange confetti in the sky,
Balloons filled with golden air,
Fly high, without a reason why,
Tickling clouds with gentle flair.

Ducks in a row, they honk and waddle,
Playing tag with the running tide,
Nature's fun, a playful nod,
In the vibrant colors wide.

Starlings put on a flashy show,
Flattering the day goodbye,
With a wink and a twinkling glow,
Silliness spreads in the sky.

Socks and sandals go on a spree,
Shopping for dreams as they drift,
Between breezy trees, oh what glee,
In the sunset's warm, funny gift.

Whispering Gardens of Gold

The daffodils share silly tales,
Of mischief done by wandering ants,
While tulips laugh, as joy prevails,
   In their colorful summer pants.

Butterflies wear tiny hats,
And play hopscotch with bumblebees,
Tickling the lilies 'neath their spats,
   In the garden's playful breeze.

Squirrels juggle acorns with flair,
   And chuckle at the setting sun,
Creating their own circus fair,
Where everyone joins in on fun.

As the golden hour draws near,
The flowers burst in laughter loud,
With giggles echoing, so clear,
A whimsical evening, oh so proud.

Shimmering Fruit Under Elysian Skies

In a grove where giggles sprout,
Fruits hang low, full of clout.
A squirrel threads through the bliss,
Swiping snacks, oh what a miss!

The trees, they sway with laughter's tone,
Bouncing sweets like a rubber cone.
A breeze tickles leaves, makes them dance,
Sweet treats roll by in a merry chance!

Fruits toss jokes in every breeze,
Juicy puns that aim to please.
The sun winks down, all cheeky bright,
In this orchard, the day's a delight!

Each bite bursts with a playful burst,
Who knew humor could quench such thirst?
In this fruity comedy, folks delight,
Under skies that shimmer just right.

Gentle Rays and Juicy Delights

The sun gabs in a soft embrace,
Laughter drips like a sunny grace.
Ripe treasures hanging from each tree,
They whisper secrets, just for me!

Cherries blushing, grinning wide,
Fruits conspire in silly pride.
Who knew juice could tickle so?
In this orchard, giggles flow!

Sunshine bubbles, sweet and clear,
Tickling noses with every cheer.
Each plump bite a comical feat,
Sugar-dusted joy, oh what a treat!

A small bird chirps its own sweet tune,
While dancing insects twirl 'neath the moon.
In every drip, a belly laugh,
Nature's joke, a fruity craft!

Essence of Afternoon Bliss

Under the sky, a canvas bright,
Fruits parade, a colorful sight.
With every bite, a chuckle sprouts,
Sweet surprise, joy, and shouts!

The breeze plays tag through a peachy rack,
Chasing giggles, it won't turn back.
A ladybug winks, cheeky and bold,
In this fruity plot, magic unfolds!

A slice of sunshine on a warm day,
Mischief blossoms in fruity play.
With sticky fingers and cheerful smirks,
Each joy-filled bite, oh how it works!

As shadows stretch and laughter swells,
Fruity tales, where happiness dwells.
A delightful charm through every smile,
The essence of joy, it's worthwhile!

The Warmth of Soft Petals

Petals dance in dazzling cheer,
Colors splash like giggles near.
A potpourri of fruity flair,
Each bloom whispers, 'Come and share!'

Honey bees buzz with playful hums,
As fruits and flowers make funny drums.
In this garden, silly gabs play,
Bloopers bloom in a bright ballet!

A bouncing berry takes a leap,
In a puddle, it starts to sleep.
With cheers around, they roll and glide,
Nature's joy can't be denied!

And when the sun begins to fade,
The echoes of laughter serenade.
In every petal, a snicker stays,
Where warmth and giggles weave all days!

Shimmering Harvest

In a grove where giggles grow,
Fruits climb trees, oh what a show!
Plump and round, they bounce around,
Shiny, slippery, on the ground.

Squirrels dance with cheeky grins,
Chasing shadows, making spins.
If you slip, just laugh and roll,
Nature's jest, a playful stroll.

Sunshine winks from leafy beams,
Toot sweet, the branch just beams!
Lumberjacks in pants so bright,
Chop the fruit in laughing fright.

Harvest smiles, a joyful cheer,
When the funny fruits come near.
So grab your basket, hold on tight,
For this feast is pure delight!

Juicy Glow of Serenity

Beneath the sun, a splash of glee,
Ripe goofballs swing from each tree.
Dripping giggles, juicy slips,
Tickled pink, with juicy quips.

Bumblebees wear tiny hats,
Buzzing 'round like chatty cats.
On cotton clouds, the laughter flows,
Where funny fruit always glows.

In the breeze, ripe tales collide,
Silly stories we can't hide.
Tickle your palate, pour some charm,
Snack on fun, there's no alarm.

A feast of laughter in every bite,
Juicy tales that dance in the light.
With every chew, the giggles sprout,
In this garden, there's no doubt!

Lustrous Tenderness

Round and plump with a wink so sly,
Jesters of the garden, oh my!
Wobbling fruit, full of delight,
Chasing shadows, what a sight!

Every bite, a burst of cheer,
Laughter spreads from ear to ear.
Cheeky smiles on every face,
Juicy frolic in this place.

Spilling sweetness, mischief flies,
Squirrels giggle, watch them rise!
They wear the blooms like flashy ties,
As sunshine plays in the skies.

Join the fun in this silly feast,
Where weird and wobbly are the least!
Savor each laugh, let spirits soar,
Tender moments are never a bore!

Flushed Charms of Twilight

As daylight fades, giggles bloom,
Fruits play tricks to fill the room.
With shadows stretched and hues awash,
A fruit parade, oh what a posh!

Silly sausages dance on the vine,
With cheeky winks, they look divine.
In twilight's glow, they shine so bright,
Drunk on laughter, what pure delight!

Tumbling to the ground with grace,
Each fruit wearing a funny face.
A banquet of whimsy, come partake,
Every slice tells a joke to make.

In the hush of the twilight's cue,
Pick your fruit, it's up to you!
Savor the joy, a taste to remember,
In this orchard, laughter's the center!

Warm Glow of Lost Moments

In the corner of my mind's clutter,
Memories dance like a playful flutter.
The sun beams down, a wink so sly,
While laughter spills like a sweet pie.

Caught between the tick-tock woes,
Chasing shadows where nobody knows.
I trip on dreams, miss the bus,
But who needs plans when it's all just fuss?

With every giggle, the world spins fast,
I reminisce on a childhood cast.
A slice of cake, a bright balloon,
In my head, it's always noon.

So here's to the blunders and silly mistakes,
With a toast of cheer for the fun that it makes.
For moments lost, yet never gone,
In the warm glow, we still carry on.

Elation of Sunkissed Revelry

The sun comes up with a gleeful shout,
Shadows and giggles, it's time to get out.
Frolic in fields where daisies twirl,
Life's a party, give joy a whirl.

With ice creams melting down my hand,
I chase little critters across the land.
A runaway kite, oh, what a sight,
These silly pranks, they feel so right.

Splash in the puddles, do not mind the mess,
Joy is a ruckus, not a game of chess.
Every splash echoes laughter so sweet,
Sun-kissed moments, oh, what a treat!

So let's toast to the sunshine's embrace,
With friends at our side, we'll keep up the pace.
The day may fade, but let's not fight,
For elation shines brightest in the twilight.

Velvet Embers of Contentment

A cozy nook with a blanket spread,
While the world outside we bravely tread.
Sipping cocoa, it's a joyful plight,
In this warmth, everything feels right.

With socks that don't match and hair a frizz,
We laugh at the chaos, a whimsical fizz.
A movie marathon, oh, what a chore,
Each scene we watch, we adore even more.

The candle flickers, tales unwind,
Every chuckle, a treasure to find.
It's in the silliness, we find our spark,
In velvet embers, joy leaves a mark.

So here's to nights of laughter and cheer,
To friendship's warmth that draws us near.
For in mischief and giggles, our hearts ignite,
Contentment found in the soft, warm light.

Sweet Resplendence of Being

Under the stars, we break into song,
With bright-eyed dreams, we all belong.
The world's a stage, we act carefree,
In this sweet moment, just you and me.

Cookies in crumbs, laughter in heaps,
We bounce through echoes, like playful leaps.
With silly hats and mismatched shoes,
In the resplendence, we can't refuse.

Plans may get tangled, that's all in the game,
But we wear our blunders like badges of fame.
With every laugh, our spirits will sing,
In this dance of joy, oh, what a fling!

So cherish the moments, however they land,
For life's comedy is perfectly planned.
In the sweetness of being, we find our note,
With hearts full of glee, on this whimsical boat.

Glistening Moments of Joy

In the garden, all things bloom,
A fuzzy fruit brings laughter's boom.
With every bite, a chuckle shared,
Juicy giggles, no one dared.

Squirrels dance in comical haste,
As juice drips down, what a taste!
Sticky fingers, messy shirts,
Nature's fun, oh how it flirts.

Oh, the sun beams like a grin,
With every snack, new giggles win.
A fruit so sweet, it knows the score,
Tickles our hearts, we ask for more.

Let's dive in without a fuss,
Creating joy, just us plus rust!
With each bright bite, we laugh and play,
Turning mundane into cabaret.

Sun-Drenched Delicacies

Under rays that dance and tease,
A fruity feast brings us to knees.
Beneath the shade, we munch with cheer,
Sunlit smiles, best times of year.

With each slice, we tell a tale,
Of summertime and wind's soft wail.
Bright colors promise silly fun,
In the laughter, we become one.

Oh, sticky pits and sugary bliss,
Makes me wonder, how could I miss?
A joyful snack, a giggle spree,
Each bite's a laugh, come share with me.

Moments like these, forever sweet,
In the park, our joy's complete.
Sunshine's hugs wrap us so tight,
Filling our days with sheer delight.

Fragrant Dawn's Caress

Mornings come with scents that tease,
A playful breeze whispers with ease.
Dewy gems on green leaves cling,
Nature's charm begins to sing.

Awake, we laugh at sleepy heads,
With dreams of treats our hearts are fed.
Each paw of the pup chases scents,
Mayhem and giggles, no pretense.

Put on your crown, it's breakfast time,
Silliness is our only rhyme.
With fluffy clouds, it's time to play,
Chasing giggles all the way.

The dawn's bright smiles paint the sky,
As we munch and howl with spry.
Life's a feast, let's make it grand,
With goofy glee as our best brand.

Golden Hour Reverie

When the world's wrapped in gold and shade,
We gather round, no plans well laid.
With laughter bubbling like sweet brew,
Every moment feels so new.

Crisp bites bring a silly cheer,
As playful friends draw near and near.
It's not just fruit, it's joy on a plate,
With every giggle, we celebrate.

As the sun dips low, we make our stance,
In this hour, we sing and dance.
Fruity antics stir up the night,
With hearts aglow, all feels right.

Let's toast with smiles and silly pranks,
In every corner, there are thanks.
With vibrant hues and humor bright,
We wrap our dreams in sheer delight.

Shimmering Essence

In the orchard, laughter grows,
Fruits giggle as the warm breeze blows.
A squirrel dances in the sun,
While birds argue over who's more fun.

Bubbles of joy in each bite,
Slippery skins that feel just right.
Buzzing bees get carried away,
Chasing shadows till the end of day.

Juices flow like stories shared,
With every bite, a slice of dared.
Sticky fingers and grinning glee,
Who knew nature could be so free?

Under the tree, we take our stance,
Watching ants in a clumsy dance.
With each chuckle, we lose our way,
In the sweet chaos of this sunny day.

Journal of Sweet Blossoms

Pages crisp with fruity cheer,
Ink spills laughter, oh so clear.
Sticky notes for silly thoughts,
Doodles of snacks and funny spots.

Every blossom shares a tale,
Of slippery slips and juicy scale.
Puns dance on petals, oh so bright,
Colors twinkle in pure delight.

Beneath the branches, mischief brewed,
Nature's pranks, we never viewed.
Picturing fruit in whimsical hats,
Bouncing thoughts like playful gnats.

With each turn of the colorful page,
Life's just a sweet, funny stage.
Nature's giggles in bloom, unfold,
Creating memories, vibrant and bold.

Lush Echoes of Clarity

In the garden, laughter roams,
Whispers of fun, tickling tomes.
The breeze tickles, a friendly punch,
As shadows play in a joyful hunch.

Fruits swing like a swing set high,
Under the watchful bluebird's eye.
Each bite bursts with silly zest,
In this realm of nature's jest.

Juggling berries, oh what a sight,
Truths revealed in a giggling light.
Juicy surprises, bubbles and cheers,
The world forgets its worries and fears.

Echoes of laughter fill the air,
As friends find joy without a care.
With every seed, a hearty laugh,
In this lush world, we take our path.

Eden's Glows of Reflection

In a meadow where chuckles play,
Silly thoughts drift like soft hay.
Reflections shimmer on the stream,
In this garden of a funny dream.

The sun flirts with the clover leaves,
Joking with shadows as it weaves.
Juicy tales roll down the hill,
With every giggle, the world stands still.

From the vines, whispers of delight,
Tickle the heart, soaring like flight.
With nature's charm, our spirits rise,
In the glow of laughter, no goodbyes.

Each moment, a dance, a silly chase,
With friends beside, we find our place.
In this Eden, humor takes lead,
Planting joy in every seed.

Honeyed Dreamscape

In a land where giggles grow,
Bumbles bounce with quite the show.
A jester's hat atop a tree,
Chasing sunbeams, wild and free.

Every fruit wears a silly grin,
Laughter bubbles as we begin.
Wobbly chairs and marshmallow pies,
Dancing squirrels with starry eyes.

Breezes that tease with a wink,
Cotton candy clouds, don't you think?
We'd share our secrets with the breeze,
While jellybeans play in the trees.

A sprinkle of joy on every stage,
Life is funny, let's disengage.
With every hug and every cheer,
A dreamscape blooms where none hold fear.

Caressed by the Sun's Embrace

Golden rays on the grassy floor,
Tickle toes, we beg for more.
Belly laughs like bouncing boats,
Silly pranks tied with brightly loats.

Stepping stones of giggling friends,
An orchestra that never ends.
Sunbaked laughter fills the air,
A wobbly dance without a care.

With every twirl, a slip, a slide,
In this joy, we take our ride.
And when the shadows start to sway,
We'll chase the giggles, come what may.

Mishaps bloom like wildflower blooms,
In this warmth where bright joy looms.
As sunbeams play and shadows tease,
Life's a jest, with such delight, please.

Radiant Shores of Memories

Waves of chuckles kiss the shore,
Seagulls joke, a playful score.
Sandcastles made of dreams and glee,
Where crabs wear hats, oh can't you see?

Shells whisper tales of beachside fun,
Ticklish toes race the setting sun.
With sunburned noses, we dive and prance,
Digging up treasures in a silly dance.

The tide brings jokes wrapped in a swirl,
Each splash a giggle, give it a twirl.
Chasing the ripples, we tumble and roll,
Seashells giggle, they're good for the soul.

Memory's tide ebbs and flows,
In every laugh, a story grows.
With whimsical winds and carefree air,
These radiant shores hold laughter rare.

Whispers in Golden Air

In a world where wonders spark,
Whispers flutter, like a lark.
Giggling leaves on the tree tops,
Soft secrets where the joy never stops.

A tickle here, a nudge over there,
Laughter spills in the gentle air.
Each breeze carries a poke and prod,
As if the sun itself plays the odd.

Silly stories woven in light,
Dancing shadows, what a sight!
We'll chase the humor, let it soar,
With every chuckle, we yearn for more.

In this golden glow, we refuge find,
Where hearts are tender, spirits unwind.
Let's dance with glee, without a care,
In whispers where joy fills the air.

Velvet Glow of Holiday Fruits

In the corner sits a bowl,
Filled with sweets to tickle the soul.
I'm convinced they wear a grin,
As I sneak a nibble, let the laughter begin!

Dancing shapes that jig and sway,
With fruity giggles, they play.
Each bite a joke, sweetened and bright,
Oh, the joy in this silly bite!

Will they share my silly fate?
Or make me slip on my plate?
With every munch and playful fling,
These merry fruits make my heart sing!

So here's to the silliness they bring,
A joyful dance, an instant zing.
Holiday treats, you're light on your toes,
In this fruity jest, hilarity grows!

The Color of Hushed Laughter.

Whispers of mischief, so sweet and bold,
With colors of fun, their stories told.
Giggles burst in hues like sun,
Oh, the joy, oh, the fun!

Tickling my senses, each vibrant shade,
Playing tricks that never fade.
They wink from the bowl with playful flair,
I think they plot, they must beware!

So we gather 'round with grins so wide,
With colorful treats, it's no place to hide.
They bounce and roll in an endless race,
Leaving trails of laughter all over the place!

In this carnival of joyful glee,
I take a bite, and a laugh sets me free.
With every chew, the hues delight,
A tasty joke, all day and night!

Sunlit Orchard Whispers

In the orchard, secrets play,
Where fruity pals meet to stray.
They chuckle softly, swinging low,
With every breeze, their giggles flow.

Branches sway with a ticklish tease,
As I sneak by, they rustle with ease.
"Oh, taste our joy!" they seem to say,
Their flavors burst in a funny display!

Each bite's a chuckle, a little surprise,
With every nibble, the laughter flies.
Dancing shadows in golden beams,
The fruit-filled fun unravels dreams!

So here I sit, amidst the cheer,
Hilarious harvest, oh dear!
In this orchard of jokes, I take my stand,
With cheerful bites, life is just grand!

Blushing Flares of Dawn

As the sun rises, hues blush and play,
In morning's warmth, they start their day.
Fruits awake with a giggle in sight,
Offering sweetness in dawn's golden light.

They stretch and sway beneath the sky,
With every rustle, a cheerful sigh.
"Grab us quick!" they seem to say,
Before the whims of the day fade away!

With each round bite, a burst of mirth,
Creating laughter right from the earth.
One snicker here, another there,
As dawn's flares dance without a care!

So let's rejoice in this morning's cheer,
With goofy grins that draw us near.
These blushing jewels, oh what a sight,
In every nibble, fun is ignited!

Warm Glow of Innocence

A fruit fell down, made quite a sound,
The giggles echoed all around.
A pit was found, a game was played,
Who knew such fun could be so laid?

Laughter bubbled like soda pop,
As silly faces made me stop.
A sticky mess with every bite,
Oh, what a joyous, sweet delight!

The sun did wink, a friendly ray,
As friends all teased in a silly way.
In every mischief, we took flight,
Chasing shadows until the night.

A warm embrace from nature's hand,
In this bright realm, we took a stand.
With every chuckle, joy arises,
Banana peels and wild surprises!

Fuzzy Chimes of Sunset

A furry fruit spun 'round and round,
Chimed like bells on merry ground.
Silly tales of how it grew,
With goofy faces, laughter flew.

On the horizon, the colors danced,
As silly squirrels with nuts pranced.
Each bump and bounce made things so bright,
We cracked up through the fading light.

The breeze would tickle, ticklish trees,
While buzzing bees buzzed just to tease.
In a whirl of fuzz, the day was done,
With every giggle, we had our fun.

With rosy blush, we'd grin and share,
Unruly moments, pure and rare.
As twilight whispered softly too,
We laughed with joy, just me and you!

Basking in Day's Warmth

Beneath the sun, we danced and played,
Chasing shadows that swiftly sway.
Hats on heads, with socks askew,
In a world where giggles grew.

With crumbs of cake upon our face,
We ran around, a merry race.
The day's embrace, so warm and bright,
Stirred up smiles like pure delight.

A splash of juice, the laughter spills,
Tickling toes with silly thrills.
As bright balloons floated by,
We caught our dreams up in the sky.

The world spun 'round in silly cheer,
While fruit-flavored jokes filled the air.
With friendships forged in golden rays,
Each joyful moment, our hearts ablaze!

Illuminated Fields of Delight

In fields of gold, we'd jump and roll,
Chasing giggles was our goal.
With fuzzy critters darting near,
The sunny air brought boundless cheer.

We played a game of tag and chase,
As shadows joined the endless race.
With every stumble, laughter soared,
In a world where fun was stored.

The sky was painted with silly hues,
As friends spun tales of wacky views.
With every grin, the world felt right,
In fields aglow, and pure delight.

Each sunset kissed the earth with glee,
As fruit and friends danced wild and free.
With hearts so light and spirits bright,
We basked together in joy's sweet sight!

Tender Glow at Dusk

In the orchard, laughter swells,
A clumsy dancer trips and yells.
Chasing shadows with a grin,
As crickets let the night begin.

Fireflies wink, a playful tease,
Buzzing round like silly bees.
Jars of jam spill on the grass,
Even the ants join in the sass.

Fruits that sparkle in the gloom,
A bumblebee zooms past my broom.
With sticky fingers, we all dive,
In this sweet chaos, we feel alive.

As we feast on nature's show,
A giggle fits, and off we go.
Dusk unveils this joyous ballet,
Where every mishap steals the day.

Sweet Fruit

Bouncing balls of fruity fun,
The best circus has begun.
Silly faces, sticky hands,
Who knew fruit could spark such plans?

Juicy laughs and wobbly bites,
Citing epic, fruit-filled fights.
A splash of juice upon your nose,
It's a comedy, goodness knows!

Fruits in funny hats parade,
The righteous peach sets the grade.
Giggles echo in the breeze,
It's a feast that aims to please.

As we munch on this delight,
Our chortles bring the stars in sight.
With every bite, the world feels right,
Join us in this fruity night!

Warm Embrace

A friend's hug feels like a pie,
Flavors swirl as we all sigh.
Laughter stitching joy so tight,
In every hug, the world feels bright.

The kitchen's filled with fragrant fun,
Baking mishaps on the run.
A sprinkle here, a splatter there,
Joy and laughter fill the air.

Through warm kisses and silly jests,
We share our tales of quirky tests.
Every smile's a slice of cheer,
In our embrace, there's nothing to fear.

With sticky hands, our hearts align,
In this warm embrace, we shall dine.
Comedy bubbles, like sweet wine,
In joyous moments, we all shine.

A Blush in the Twilight

Twilight tints the world anew,
Where giggles burst and banter grew.
Chasing shadows, we all race,
A blush spreads wide on every face.

Marshmallows roast like silly clouds,
We embark amid silly crowds.
With sticky fingers and charred ends,
We're the unusual, fun-filled friends.

The fruits present a cheeky dare,
Juggling while we munch and share.
As laughter dances on the breeze,
Truth or dare? Just share the cheese!

In twilight's glow, the shenanigans thrive,
With every giggle, we come alive.
Beneath the stars, our spirits soar,
In this silly game, who could ask for more?

Warmth of the Harvest

Gather round for tales to spin,
Fall bounty makes the laughter win.
Covered in flavors, sweet and bold,
In every hug, stories unfold.

Laughter peels like ripe fruit skin,
In this harvest, we dive right in.
Our basket overflows with cheer,
Even pumpkins giggle here.

The sun dips low, a joke is cracked,
We tumble down, our chill distracts.
With cider spills and silly dances,
Joy springs forth in wild romances.

In every bite, warmth awakens,
And funny tales, our hearts have taken.
As the night swirls in with delight,
We harvest giggles, pure and bright.

Enchanted Gaze of Day

The sun peeks in, a cheeky grin,
While shadows dance, let the fun begin!
With laughter near, and winks so sly,
It tickles the leaves, as birds fly by.

The clock's confused, tick-tock it sways,
Time's on break, in such silly ways!
Giggles escape, from all around,
As fruity dreams bounce off the ground.

Jellybeans drip from the sweet trees' ends,
And everyone here just pretends!
To sip the joy from springtime wells,
In a world that's spun with laughter spells.

So smile, dear friend, in this bright embrace,
Where the wacky moments leave quite the trace!
Brush off your woes and dance a bit,
For golden mischief stays true and lit!

Drenched in Honey Glow

Slip and slide, in the warmest bliss,
With every giggle adding to this!
A sticky splatter, oh what a sight,
As friends fall down, laughing in delight.

Golden drizzles from the silly skies,
Create ruckus, oh how it flies!
A sprinkle here, a dabble there,
Not a care, life's beyond compare.

Bumbles bounce on the murky ground,
In crooked lines, they race around!
The more they trip, the brighter the cheer,
It's honeyed chaos, never fear!

So let's pour giggles, like syrupy streams,
And dance with joy in our daydreams!
Who knew fun could be this glowy?
In this sweet world, we're never lowey!

Soft Glimmers of Innocence

Whispers float on a gentle breeze,
Where giggles tease, and minds are at ease.
A cuddle here, a tickle there,
In playful circles, we twirl without care.

The carousels spin with youthful zeal,
Round and round, let's seal the deal!
With sprightly hops and candy chats,
We share our dreams like curious cats.

Invisible pranks on the world outside,
Where frowns retreat, and joy's the guide.
A wink exchanged, let's run and flee,
The treasures await, just you and me.

So toss your hat to the gleeful sky,
As giggles soar and worries go shy!
In this land of blasts from the past,
We hold the fun, forever to last!

Dappled Fields of Perception

Sunshiny patches dance on the ground,
Where silly shenanigans can be found!
A hopscotch of thoughts, bouncing around,
With chortles and snorts, astoundingly sound.

Every truth is now twisted and spun,
In fields of whimsy, two times the fun!
Shapes turn to giggles as whispers fly,
While trees throw shade with a twinkling eye.

The air's akimbo, it sways with glee,
Shipping odd ideas like wild-flavored tea.
A frolicsome mess, where nonsense reigns,
Our smiles bloom like wild, wacky gains.

So prance with delight, through the quirky path,
And chase the bubble of silly math!
In this frothy realm of absurdity,
We embrace the charm, in purest clarity!

Glowing Embers of Deliciousness

In the orchard, fruit giggles loud,
As fuzzy spheres dance in a crowd.
They bounce around, oh what a sight,
Spreading joy, from morning to night.

A plump one slips, falls on the ground,
Rolling away, a merry-go-round.
With each bounce, they tease and play,
Saying, "Catch me if you may!"

Their sweetness hangs, a candy dream,
Best enjoyed with a splashy scream.
Sticky fingers, a glorious mess,
Crowned with laughter, oh what a bless!

As the sun sets, they glow like stars,
Filling the air with fragrant jars.
Who knew dessert could be so fun?
In this fruity world, we've just begun!

Nature's Silken Touch

In the meadow, berries prance,
Playing games, they steal a glance.
With every breeze, they flip and swirl,
Nature's jesters in a twirl.

A breeze whispers secrets so sweet,
Tickling leaves, a playful feat.
The sun chimes in with its warm embrace,
A slapstick show in a green space.

Wobbling fruit, oh what a show,
Rolling down the hill, oh no, oh no!
Laughter echoes, like birds in flight,
As nature shares its soft delight.

With each chuckle, the colors bloom,
And mischief fills every room.
Sipping sunlight, oh what a clutch,
In the garden, we feel its touch.

Dreaming in Floral Glow

A fruit falls down from branches high,
With a giggle, it gives a sigh.
It dreams of thrones and fancy feasts,
While bees buzz by, like roaming beasts.

Petals dance in the evening air,
Whispering jokes without a care.
Blushing blooms with petals bright,
Twirl and swirl in the fading light.

Fruitful fantasies take their flight,
Tickled by jokes, what a sight!
When twilight falls, they laugh aloud,
Creating shadows, a jester's crowd.

Each little bud bursts into song,
Celebrating where they belong.
In floral dreams, the world's aglow,
With laughter echoing, 'Oh, let's go!'

Sun-Drenched Sweetness

The sun shines bright, a golden beam,
Fruits bask in warmth, living the dream.
They giggle as they soak and sip,
Whirling around in a juicy trip.

A squirrel shows off his acrobatic flair,
As berries bounce, without a care.
With sun-drenched cheer and playful tease,
Everyone joins in the sun's warm breeze.

Sticky smiles and gleeful shouts,
Eating berries, there's no doubts.
Chasing shadows, playing tag,
Tumbling down in a happy gag.

As sunset glimmers, colors blend,
The fruity frolic will never end.
With laughter rising in blissful waves,
We dance under skies, our laughter saves!

Sweet Amber Horizon

Under the glow, we laugh and play,
Chasing the jokes as they dance away.
Fruit-flavored giggles fill the air,
Tickling our hearts without a care.

Beneath the trees with taffy leaves,
We trade our stories, nobody grieves.
Laughter rings out like a summer breeze,
Sticky fingers, sweet as honey bees.

With every bite, the world feels bright,
Even the squirrels join in our delight.
Sunshine drips from the branches high,
Tickling our toes, like a happy sigh.

In this bright space where joy's our game,
Every silly riddle whispers your name.
We hop and skip, no care in sight,
Under the charm of this golden night.

Radiant Splendor Unfurled

In fields of fun where smiles abound,
We dance like fools on joyful ground.
Sprinkling laughter with every step,
Mischief blooms as we boldly prep.

With shades of joy painting our day,
The sun winks back in a cheeky way.
Juggling memories, we share a grin,
Giggles bloom like the finest din.

Pranks and puns float in the breeze,
Chasing our shadows, giggling with ease.
The air's alive, a playful tease,
Turning our worries into a cheese.

So let's toast to a world so grand,
Where silliness is always at hand.
Champagne laughter, we sip and swirl,
Under the magic of fun's bright whirl.

Honeyed Curves of Reflection

Mirror, mirror, on the floor,
Who's the silliest of them all?
We giggle at faces all askew,
Prompting the shadows to join our crew.

Reflections twist in a delightful dance,
As we spin in a silly trance.
Our joy spills over, bright and round,
Chortles and snorts echo all around.

Catch the moments as they fly,
Tickled pink, we leap and try.
In this realm where laughter reigns,
Every slip brings golden gains.

So let's skip stones and paint the air,
With jokes that swirl and wiggle like hair.
In the stillness of sweet, bright hues,
We wrap our hearts in laughter's muse.

Dappled Sunlit Secrets

Under the shady, spotted veil,
Whispers of jesting tales prevail.
The light plays tricks, like a nimble sprite,
Chasing our giggles into the night.

With every flicker, a smile sparks,
As secrets tangle with cheeky remarks.
Sunbeams chuckle, casting their tease,
While we frolic through joys that please.

Frothy bubbles of laughter ignite,
Puffing up dreams in glowing light.
Little secrets tucked in the sun,
Making mischief, oh what fun!

So here we stand, hearts full and free,
Under the play of this comedy.
With each twinkle like joy unfurled,
We scamper on, our giggles swirled.

www.ingramcontent.com/pod-product-compliance
Lightning Source LLC
Chambersburg PA
CBHW070002300426
43661CB00141B/151